VICTORIA

Victoria is a Garden State, fertile and prosperous, with an abundance of natural wonders and a wealth of history. Melbourne, its capital, is one of the world's great cities.

Melbourne was founded in 1835 and proclaimed Victoria's capital city in 1851. Soon afterwards, gold discoveries brought great riches and hordes of immigrants to the colony. Many remained in Victoria after leaving the goldfields, contributing their skills and establishing the multiculturalism for which the State is noted to this day. Today Victoria's capital is a vibrant, vital metropolis, a centre of culture and commerce whose historic beauties are complemented by stunning modern constructions.

Victoria is about 780 km from east to west. Its 227,600 km^2 area embraces a wide variety of memorable landscapes, from the rugged, snow-capped mountains of the Great Divide in the north-east to the temperate forests of the Otway Ranges and the arid plains of the north-west.

To the north, most of the State border is formed by the mighty Murray, a magnificent river that supplies water for orchards and vineyards and can be travelled in style in vessels ranging from rafts to paddlesteamers.

To the south, the coastline is wondrously varied. Two fine harbours, Port Phillip Bay and Western Port, are in the centre. To their east are granite headlands, sandy beaches and coastal lakes. To their west are world-class surf beaches, secluded coves and the spectacular cliffs and stacks of Port Campbell National Park, accessible from the Great Ocean Road.

Victoria is the smallest mainland Australian State, proof of the old saying that good things come in small packages. Within easy reach of Melbourne are explorations, adventures and experiences that make Victoria a joy to visit.

Steve Parish
PUBLISHING

Top: *Melbourne tram passing Flinders Street Station.* **Above:** *(Left) Statue of poet Adam Lindsay Gordon in Spring Street.*
(Right) Melbourne is a pedestrian-friendly city. This is one of the entrances to Bourke Street Mall.
Opposite: *An aerial view of Melbourne with St Paul's Cathedral in the foreground.*

MELBOURNE: VICTORIA'S CAPITAL

Melbourne is one of the world's most enjoyable places to visit, easy to reach by road or train and a delight to explore on foot, or riding one of the city's famous trams. Victoria's capital is rich in parks and gardens and its wide, tree-lined streets complement historic buildings which are legacies from the gold, wool and timber booms of the nineteenth century. The Yarra River runs through the city's heart, down to the busy docks of Port Melbourne before flowing into the wide waters of Port Phillip Bay. Australia's second largest city is a dynamic commercial centre, but a city where quality of life is valued, and whose cosmopolitan residents welcome visitors. It is full of charm, gracious and hospitable.

MELBOURNE'S YARRA RIVER

As the Yarra River wanders towards Port Phillip Bay, it winds through Melbourne's suburbs and business centre, passing under many bridges and through some of the city's loveliest parklands. Melburnians, and visitors to the city, find many ways to enjoy the Yarra. They cycle along its banks, play sport and picnic in a wealth of green spaces. From dawn to dusk, its placid surface is host to people enjoying themselves in canoes, kayaks, cruise vessels, racing shells and even gondolas.

Top: *(Left) A gondola floats towards Princes Bridge. (Right) The Yarra is a training ground for rowers.*
Centre: *Westgate Bridge.* **Above:** *A lone sculler on the Yarra at dawn.* **Opposite:** *The Yarra River in the early morning.*

Top: (Left) The Crown Entertainment Complex and casino. (Right) The magnificent Melbourne Aquarium. **Centre:** The footbridge from Southgate to Flinders Walk. **Above:** (Left to right) The spire of the Theatres Building of the Victorian Arts Centre; Deborah Halpern's sculpture Ophelia at Southgate; Polly Woodside, a beautifully restored three-masted barque built in 1855, is moored outside the Melbourne Exhibition Centre on the Yarra. **Opposite:** Entertaining the crowds at Southgate.

ON YARRA'S BANKS

Southgate, on the south bank of the Yarra, has some of Melbourne's most delightful places to eat and relax, from exclusive restaurants to the popular crush of the Wharf Food Market. Just down-river is the Crown Entertainment Complex and the marvellous Melbourne Aquarium, where visitors can wander through displays of fantastic fish and other marine life. This is a must-visit place.

Adjacent to Southgate, the Arts Precinct is home to the Victorian Arts Centre, the Melbourne Concert Hall, the Victorian College of the Arts and the internationally recognised National Gallery of Victoria. A reminder that the Yarra ends in a busy port, the *Polly Woodside*, a beautifully restored three-masted barque built in 1855 is moored outside the Melbourne Exhibition Centre on the Yarra.

Above: *Flinders Street Station, built on the site of an earlier terminus, was completed in 1910. It is a hub for Victoria's suburban railway network.*
Below: *(Left) St Paul's Cathedral was built between 1877 and 1891, but its towers were not added until 1931.*
(Right) The Princess Theatre was a product of the nineteenth-century gold rush days. Built in 1854, it has been restored to its former opulence.

Above: *The Shrine of Remembrance was erected to honour Victorians who died in World War I. Its design echoes that of one of the Seven Wonders of the World, the Mausoleum at Helicarnassus. The forecourt features an eternal flame.*

MELBOURNE ICONS

Melbourne has been described as the greatest living example of a Victorian (nineteenth century) city. Many of its imposing historic buildings date to the gold-fuelled boom times of the second half of the 1800s. When later generations added their own grand edifices, they continued for many years to erect monumental stone walls crowned with spires or domes. No matter how spectacular the glass-walled towers of the modern city additions, it is these older buildings, born from Old World traditions, that have become Melbourne's most-admired city icons. The Shrine of Remembrance, completed in 1934, is a stately and moving tribute to classical Greek architecture.

Top: *(Left) Charming modern artwork by Deborah Halpern in the Royal Botanic Gardens. (Right) Enjoying the Royal Botanic Gardens.* **Above:** *An aerial view of the Royal Botanic Gardens.* **Opposite: Top:** *(Left) A cascade in Fitzroy Gardens, a park originally designed in 1857. (Right) Government House stands in Kings Domain. Ready for occupation in 1876, it is considered one of Australia's finest buildings of the Italianate style.* **Centre:** *(Left) A bronze sculpture, by W. Leslie-Bowles, of the Greek goddess Diana and her hounds graces an entrance to Fitzroy Gardens' Conservatory. (Right) This Lowland Gorilla is a member of a breeding group at Royal Melbourne Zoo.* **Bottom:** *(Left) A magnificent floral display in the Conservatory, Fitzroy Gardens. (Right) Captain James Cook's parents' cottage was transported from England and reconstructed in Fitzroy Gardens in 1934.*

A CITY OF GARDENS

Melbourne's early city planners took advantage of the fertile lowlands bordering the Yarra and laid out a city graced by many public parks and gardens. A kindly climate, with abundant winter rain and warm summers, fostered European plantings. Today's Melbourne has parks to suit every need, from the jigsaw garden beds and waterfowl-haunted ponds of the Royal Botanic Gardens to the grandeur of Kings Domain and the sculpture-rich, Yarra-side Queen Victoria Gardens. The splendid Royal Melbourne Zoo, third oldest in the world, is deservedly popular with locals and visitors. It is particularly well-known for its breeding groups of endangered animals, such as gorillas.

Above: *Melbourne Central's conical dome, the biggest glass cone in the world, rises 20 storeys high and houses the historic Shot Tower, built in 1889.*

Below: *(Left to right) The giant fob watch inside Melbourne Central dome has unexpected secrets; Melbourne Central also houses a busy shopping and business complex; 234 Collins Street is a wonderland for serious shoppers; the figures of Gog and Magog have stood sentinel in the Royal Arcade, Bourke Street, since 1892.*

Top: (Left) Lygon Street, in the inner suburb of Carlton, has a long tradition of offering the best in cosmopolitan food.
(Right) Little Bourke Street, the place to find excellent Chinese restaurants, as well as good food from many other nations.
Above: (Left) Entrance to Ian Potter Gallery, Federation Square. (Right) History buffs and those who enjoy a chill down the spine can investigate the grim exhibits at the Old Melbourne Gaol.

OUT AND ABOUT IN MELBOURNE

There is much to do in Melbourne. Those who love to shop can indulge themselves in many ways, from take-no-prisoners expeditions to boutiques and department stores, to browsing around book and antique shops or plunging into the glorious hurley-burley of the Queen Victoria Market.

For culture, the Arts Precinct offers the stunning Victorian National Gallery and the Victorian Arts Centre, and smaller theatres and galleries are scattered throughout city and suburbs. There's a whole world to be discovered while exploring historic Melbourne, with one of the recommended attractions being Old Melbourne Gaol which is haunted by ghostly memories of convicts and executions, not least that of bushranger Ned Kelly.

PORT PHILLIP BAY

Melbourne's central business district stands about five kilometres from where the Yarra River enters Port Phillip Bay. The bay, which is enclosed by the Bellarine Peninsula on the west and the Mornington Peninsula on the east, is an ocean in miniature, its moods influenced by those of Bass Strait outside its entrance. The narrow opening between Point Lonsdale and Point Nepean is a place of swirling and sometimes dangerous currents, which form a turbulence known as The Rip.

Suburbs extend down both sides of the bay. Near-city ones, such as St Kilda and Williamstown, are popular places to eat out and keep a small boat moored. Further from the city, on the Mornington Peninsula in particular, seaside resorts are becoming commuter suburbs during weekdays. At the weekend, they attract visitors to fish, swim, sail, sailboard, surf and generally enjoy the seaside.

Top: *The multi-coloured bathing boxes at Brighton, peaceful in winter but centres of activity in warmer weather.*
Above: *(Left) Sailboarding on Port Phillip Bay. (Right) Port Phillip Bay is a playground right on Melbourne's doorstep.*

Above: *Vessels moored at Williamstown.* **Below:** *(Left) Fishing and walking are popular occupations at St Kilda and other bay piers.* *(Right) A birdseye view of the children's activity centre at the fascinating Scienceworks Museum, a popular attraction in Spotswood, near the mouth of the Yarra.*

The Melbourne Cricket Ground (MCG) is easily identified from across the Yarra River.

MELBOURNE – A SPORTING CITY

Melbourne is paradise for sportspeople and spectators. It is the headquarters of Australian Rules Football, played between April and September and dreamed about by its fans for the rest of the year. The national competition includes 16 teams, 10 from Victoria. The Melbourne Cricket Ground hosts Australian Rules games during winter and cricket for the rest of the year. Colonial Stadium is also a first-class sporting facility, which sees its share of top fixtures.

Melbourne also boasts a world-class tennis facility, the National Tennis Centre at Melbourne Park, at which the Australian Open is held each January. The Australian leg of the international Formula One Grand Prix is raced at the Albert Park course each year and the World 500cc Motorcycle Grand Prix is held at Phillip Island.

But the event which undoubtedly captures world attention, and which "stops Australia" on the first Tuesday of every November, is the Melbourne Cup, at Flemington Racecourse. The Cup has moved far beyond being just a horse-race and is now a national institution.

Above: *And they're racing in Australia's richest horse-race, the Melbourne Cup, at Flemington Racecourse.*
Below: *Prematch entertainment for the capacity crowd at the AFL Grand Final at the MCG (Melbourne Cricket Ground), also known as The G.*

Top: *Point Nepean National Park, Fort Nepean and The Rip guard the entrance to Port Phillip.* **Above:** *Cape Schanck, the southernmost prominence on the Bass Strait aspect of the peninsula.*

THE MORNINGTON PENINSULA

The comparatively sheltered "front beaches" of the Mornington Peninsula face Port Phillip Bay. The "back beaches" confront the surf of Bass Strait. The peninsula's northern towns are rapidly becoming outlying suburbs of Melbourne, but those most distant from the city retain their seaside charm and are great places to relax, swim, sail and go fishing. There are bush and seaside walks, great views from Arthur's Seat on the spine of the peninsula inland from Dromana and, for wine buffs, the pleasures of sampling vintages from the peninsula's excellent wineries.

Above: *Cabin cruisers moored in a peninsula bay.* **Below:** *(Left) Hastings Boat Harbour, on the eastern side of the peninsula on Western Port Bay. (Right) Sorrento Back Beach.*

Top: *Healesville has a flourishing colony of Koalas.* **Above:** *(Left) Eastern Pygmy-possum. (Right) Platypus.*

HEALESVILLE WILDLIFE SANCTUARY

Sixty-five kilometres from Melbourne off the Maroondah Highway is Healesville Wildlife Sanctuary, famous for breeding the rare Platypus and other native animals and for its comprehensive collection of Australian fauna. There are walk-through areas for closer contact between visitors and residents, picnic facilities, and special presentations such as the free-flying birds of prey.

Though of modest height (Mt Dandenong is 633 m), the Dandenong Ranges are cool and wet enough to harbour magnificent gardens that provide colourful displays of autumn leaves and gorgeous gardens of bulbs and rhododendrons in springtime. Stands of tall Mountain Ash, descendants of trees which felt the loggers' axes in the nineteenth century, tower over gullies of tree ferns. In less disturbed areas, male Superb Lyrebirds still perform their song and dance routines, shimmering their silvery plumes to attract females and to discourage rivals.

Top: *(Left) Male Superb Lyrebird. (Right) Magnificent rhododendrons star in this Dandenong garden.* **Above:** *Puffing Billy runs between Belgrave and Emerald Lakeside Park four times each week day, and adds Gembrook to its route on weekends.*

Top: *(Left) Phillip Island coast. (Left) A Little Penguin heads for its burrow.* **Above:** *(Left) The Nobbies stand off the south-west extremity of Phillip Island. Beyond them lie Seal Rocks. (Right) Australia's largest colony of Australian Fur-seals lives on Seal Rocks. The seals breed from October to December.* **Opposite:** *Cape Woolamai, on Phillip Island's south-east extremity.*

PHILLIP ISLAND

Scenic Phillip Island is 120 km south-east of Melbourne by road and connected to the mainland by a bridge stretching from Newhaven to San Remo. It is a wonderful place for a holiday – the calm beaches on its Western Port side are ideal for families, and on its Bass Strait side are some of the best surf beaches in Victoria. Fishing, sailing, walking, and relaxing are other island pastimes.

However, many people would count their visit to Phillip Island well worth while if they only saw the just-after-sunset arrival of Little Penguins. After a day's fishing at sea, these flightless little birds waddle from the surf up the beach to their nests. In summer, their crops are full of fish for their chicks. Close-up views of other fascinating creatures can be had by taking a cruise to see the Australian Fur-seals on Seal Rocks, or by visiting the island's Koala Conservation Centre.

THE BELLARINE PENINSULA

The Bellarine Peninsula is the western arm enclosing Port Phillip Bay. Victoria's largest provincial city, Geelong, stands on Corio Bay at the north of the peninsula, where the Hamilton Highway begins its run west through the fertile wool- and wheat-producing Western District.

The Bellarine Highway runs down the centre of the peninsula to Queenscliff, originally a base for the marine pilots who guided ships through the dangerous rip between Point Lonsdale and Point Nepean at the narrow entrance to the bay. Construction of Fort Queenscliff was begun in 1863 because of fears of a Russian invasion. Today it houses the Australian Army Command and Staff College. Queenscliff's beautifully restored nineteenth century hotels, cafés and restaurants make it a popular get-away, with the added attraction of the ferry to Sorrento on the Mornington Peninsula.

Top: *(Left) Fountain at Corio Bay, Geelong. (Right) Jan Mitchell's Baywalk Bollards — 104 timber statues providing a chronicle of Geelong.* **Above:** *Sunlight burnishes Port Phillip Bay, Geelong.* **Opposite:** *(Top) Marine Discovery Centre, Queenscliff — a great facility for learning about the marine environment of southern Australia. (Bottom) Black Lighthouse, Fort Queenscliff.*

Top: *(Left to right) Point Addis; Anglesea; Torquay.* **Above:** *(Left to right) Lorne; Aireys Inlet, with Split Point Lighthouse in the distance.* **Opposite:** *Aerial view of the Great Ocean Road near Lorne.*

THE GREAT OCEAN ROAD

In spite of the nineteenth century demand for timber and land, for many years Victoria's south-western coastal settlements, which could have met the demand, could be reached only by sea. After World War I, thousands of returned soldiers were employed to build a coastal highway, using picks, shovels and crowbars. The Great Ocean Road was opened in 1932, a magnificent engineering achievement and a memorial to the men who laboured on it.

In the 1980s, the section of winding dirt road which stretched across Cape Otway was straightened and sealed, connecting the coastal roads on either side of the cape. Today, the renovated Great Ocean Road is one of the world's great scenic coastal drives, linking seaside resorts and giving breathtaking views of spectacular cliffs, islands, stacks and an ever-changing sea. It gives access to not only stunning coastal views but also to the green splendours of the temperate rainforests of south-western Victoria.

THE OTWAY RANGES

The Otways stretch from between Anglesea and Aireys Inlet to Cape Otway, and their high rainfall, rich soils and temperate climate have fostered marvellous forests, picturesque streams, waterfalls and a wealth of wildlife. Loggers ravaged their magnificence until the third quarter of the twentieth century, but Melba State Park was proclaimed in 1975 and Otway National Park in 1981. Angahook-Lorne State Park was protected in 1987. Today, all these reserves are wonderful places to visit.

Top: (Left to right) Beauchamp Falls in the Otway Ranges; Eastern Grey Kangaroo and joey; Eastern Yellow Robin. **Above:** Tree ferns and creek in Melba Gully State Park. **Opposite:** Erskine Falls, a much-visited beauty spot in Angahook-Lorne State Park.

Top: *An aerial view of "the indented coast", showing Mutton Bird Island on the right.* **Above:** *(Left) London Bridge. (Right) Loch Ard Gorge.* **Opposite:** *The Twelve Apostles, a group of limestone stacks off the Port Campbell National Park coast.*

PORT CAMPBELL NATIONAL PARK

A stunningly scenic stretch of the Great Ocean Road runs for 32 kilometres through Port Campbell National Park, where limestone cliffs drop sheer to the Southern Ocean. Surging waves undercut these cliffs, creating caves which collapse to leave isolated columns known as stacks. The Twelve Apostles are the best-known of these formations, but London Bridge, Mutton Bird Island, the Bakers Oven and the Grotto are others. Loch Ard Gorge, where 52 people lost their lives when, in 1878, the three-masted clipper *Loch Ard* was swept onto a reef extending from Mutton Bird Island, is only one of many shipwreck sites.

Boardwalks and platforms allow splendid views for sightseers and tracks lead down to sheltered bays and magical little beaches, where Little Penguins may be seen at dusk and dawn.

Top: *A morning view from Mt William.* **Above:** *(Left to right) Grampians landmarks: The Balconies; Silent Street; The Pinnacle; Brambuk — The National Park and Cultural Centre.* **Opposite:** *MacKenzie Falls is one of the Grampians' loveliest cascades.*

THE GRAMPIANS

The peaks and ridges of the Grampians rise from south-western Victoria's grazing lands and look northwards to grain farms and the Mallee country. Their sandstones and granites form a wide variety of landscapes, with rugged rock formations overlooking softly rounded hills and placid lakes. They are home to an incredible array of plants and wildlife, protected by the area's national park status. Rock-climbers, bush-walkers and nature-lovers find the Grampians richly rewarding. The area has a long Aboriginal heritage, celebrated today at Brambuk — The National Park and Cultural Centre.

THE WIMMERA AND THE MALLEE

The area which surrounds the Grampians is known as the Wimmera. It is a fertile region noted for wheat and sheep and takes its name from *wimare*, the Aboriginal word for the Wimmera River and its tributaries. Besides the Grampians, the region is noted for Mt Arapiles, which attracts rock-climbers from all over the world, the historic gold-rush towns of Ararat and Stawell (home of the rich Stawell Gift foot-race), and the Little Desert National Park.

North of the Wimmera is the Mallee, named after a drought-resistant eucalypt with many slender trunks. Mallee woodlands once covered large areas of the arid north-western corner of Victoria, but in many places have been replaced by wheat and sheep properties. This is a land of wide spaces, where birdwatchers and admirers of wildflowers are richly rewarded in springtime. The remarkable Mallee Fowl, which incubates its many eggs in a nest mound of sand and vegetation, is a rare and endangered inhabitant of this region.

Top: *(Left) A Mallee Fowl on its nest mound. (Right) Mt Arapiles is a rockclimber's heaven.* **Above:** *(Left) Emus in Mallee country. (Right) Wildflowers blossom in the Mallee after rain.* **Opposite:** *(Top) Years ago, Aborigines removed a section of bark from this tree in Wyperfeld National Park, possibly to make a traditional canoe. (Bottom) Cereal crops are grown in drier western Victoria.*

Top: *The placid Murray River forms the border between two States. This scene is near Mildura.* **Above:** *The Sturt Highway connects Victoria to New South Wales across this bridge at Mildura.* **Opposite:** *(Top) The paddlewheeler* Avoca, *fully restored and based at Echuca. (Bottom, left to right) A nineteenth-century paddlewheeler; the Pevensey at historic Echuca wharf.*

THE MURRAY RIVER

The Murray River can be traced to a source near Mt Kosciuszko. It flows from the Great Dividing Range across fertile plains, in a 2500 km journey. Most of the Murray's course across Victoria can be traced along the Murray Valley Highway that follows the river from Corryong in the foothills of the Australian Alps, westward to Robinvale. From there, the road skirts Hattah-Kulkyne National Park to Mildura, and the Sturt Highway goes on to the South Australian border. For much of the 1800s, riverboats transported passengers, wool, timbers and other goods down the Murray. Echuca was Australia's leading inland port and as many as 16 vessels and their barges could be unloaded at once at the port's famous red-gum wharf. Today Echuca and other Murray towns provide glimpses of the roaring riverboat days, and exploring the river by paddlewheeler, houseboat, canoe or raft is popular.

Top: *(Left) Mt Hotham is a popular winter resort. (Right) Mt Buffalo attracts rockclimbers.* **Above:** *(Left) The Snow Gum is the only tree to survive above the snowline. (Right) Common Wombats live in the High Country.* **Opposite:** *(Top) Mt Feathertop, Alpine National Park. (Bottom) The High Country in summer.*

THE HIGH COUNTRY

Victoria's spectacular alpine region is popularly known as the High Country. Although not excessively lofty (Mt Bogong, at 1986 m, is the highest peak), the region offers great snow sports in winter and is a magnet for anglers, bushwalkers and other active people in summer. Two national parks, Alpine and Mt Buller, protect the fragile alpine environment and co-exist with ski resorts.

The main resorts are Mt Buller (around 220 km from Melbourne), Mt Buffalo (about 330), Falls Creek (about 350) and Mt Hotham (about 365). The skiing season opens in early June and closes in October. Then the High Country emerges from its white mantle and shines in summer greens and golds, luring a new group of adventurers to sample its delights.

THE GOLD TRAIL

In 1851, gold was discovered at Warrandyte, Ballarat and Bendigo, and Victoria became the focus of treasure-hunters from all over the world. Wealth poured into the colony's economy and by the 1880s the gold towns, and the city of Melbourne, were enriched by magnificent buildings and hugely increased populations. Today Ballarat and Bendigo and surrounding districts and towns are full of relics of the gold rush days, including public buildings and artworks that were funded by the wealth of those golden days. Ballarat offers a time-warp experience in the recreated 1860s gold rush town of Sovereign Hill. The notorious 1854 rebellion of miners against an unjust licensing system is commemorated at the town's Eureka Stockade Centre.

Top: (Left) Cobb & Co coach, Sovereign Hill. (Right) Gold-era fountain, Daylesford. **Centre:** (Left) An opulent gold-rush fountain in Bendigo. (Right) Horseman, Sovereign Hill. **Above:** Ballarat Mining Exchange.

NED KELLY

Ned Kelly was born in 1855 and hanged in Old Melbourne Gaol in 1880. His short life spanned years when gold-earned prosperity ensured that there would be two thousand pounds (a great sum for the time) in the bank at Euroa to be robbed by the Kelly Gang in 1878, and that rewards of the same sum could be offered for Ned, his brother Dan, Steve Hart and Joe Byrne. The gang held 60 hostages in the Glenrowan Hotel, where they were besieged by police. Three of them died, and armour-wearing Ned was captured and carried off to Melbourne for trial. A legend was born.

Above: (Left) Courthouse, Steiglitz Historical Park. (Right) The Organ Pipes, Organ Pipes National Park.

CLOSE TO MELBOURNE

Victoria is rich in places of scenic and historic interest, many of them easily reached from Melbourne. Steiglitz Historical Park, midway between Ballarat and Geelong, is typical of many fascinating memorials to colonial days. The basalt Organ Pipes, which occupy a small national park just off the Calder Highway, a short drive from Melbourne, are a charming example of the State's scenic riches.

Top: *Autumn burnishes a garden at Bright.* **Above:** *Autumn deciduous trees in north-eastern Victoria.* **Opposite:** *(Top) Ancient beech forest at Marysville, north-east of Melbourne. (Bottom left) Marysville stream. (Bottom right) Crimson Rosella.*

TREES – EXOTIC AND NATIVE

Victoria's early settlers planted the trees they knew and loved "back home" in Europe and later generations have also favoured deciduous trees that change their leaves to reds and golds as autumn progresses then renew their foliage in spring. However, in high rainfall areas of the State where logging and clearing have been controlled, majestic native forests of ancient beech and towering stands of Mountain Ash and other tall trees still remain. They harbour native wildlife, including some endangered species, and it is to be hoped they will be protected for future generations to marvel at.

Top: *Enjoying the view from Mt Oberon.* **Centre:** *The sands of Squeaky Beach sing under bare feet.* **Above:** *(Left to right) Lilly Pilly Gully Nature Walk; Whisky Bay; Whale Rock.* **Opposite:** *A lighthouse stands on South East Point.*

WILSONS PROMONTORY

Yanakie, about 170 km from Melbourne, stands at the entry point to Wilsons Promontory, a national park since 1905. The park's information centre at Tidal River is 32 km along the Nature Drive from the entrance. The Prom is a magnificent place of abundant wildlife, rugged headlands, sandy beaches, flowering heathland and rainforest gullies, of particular appeal to naturalists and bushwalkers. There are stunning views across Bass Strait from Mt Oberon and Sparkes Lookout and more than 100 km of walking tracks, some short, some for only the fit.

THE LAKES AND GIPPSLAND

The fertile coastal lowlands of Gippsland, in Victoria's central south-east, provide endless opportunities for exploration and enjoyment. The area includes Australia's largest system of internal waterways, wonderful beaches, rolling green pastures on which graze dairy and beef herds, and historic townships. The Lakes are popular with holiday-makers and nature-lovers and there are plenty of opportunities for sailing, bushwalking, fishing, birdwatching or just relaxing in beautiful surroundings. The major towns of the area are Bairnsdale, Lakes Entrance, Paynesville and Metung. Rotamah Island is a destination for birdwatchers, while in Mitchell River Park, a short drive north-west of Bairnsdale, is found the Den of Nargun, a half-stone creature of Aboriginal legend.

Top: (Left) Paynesville, a popular centre near Lake Victoria. (Right) Lifesavers on Ninety Mile Beach.
Above: Lakes Entrance is a break in a gigantic sand bar, Ninety Mile Beach, which separates the Gippsland Lakes from the ocean.

Top: *The Den of Nargun, Mitchell River National Park.* **Above:** *(Left) The view from Genoa Peak, Croajingolong National Park. (Right) This obelisk at Point Hicks records the sighting of the Australian mainland by one of Captain Cook's crew, Lieutenant Hicks.* **Page 48:** *(Top to bottom) The Twelve Apostles; the Western Districts; the dry north-west; the Victorian High Country.*

GIPPSLAND'S SOUTH-EAST

Gippsland's extreme south-east has largely remained a wilderness. It is an area of unspoiled coasts and inlets, and features four fine national parks. Croajingolong National Park is coastal, Snowy River is mountainous and continues over the border as Kosciuszko National Park, Errinundra is notable for rainforest, and Coopracambra National Park, largely undiscovered by travellers, is a wilderness region featuring the spectacular Genoa Gorge. The major centres for the south-east of Gippsland are Orbost, on the western approach to the region, and Mallacoota, in the extreme north-east.